Building Character & Community in the Classroom K–3

Written by

Ronda Howley

Melissa Mangan

Katie Oplawski

Jody Vogel

Editor:

Joellyn Thrall Cicciarelli

Illustrator:

Darcy Tom

Project Director:

Carolea Williams

Table of Contents

A caring classroom community consists of happy, confident students led by a strong, nurturing teacher. *Building Character & Community in the Classroom* offers creative activities to build a sense of community among your students through the development of positive character traits. The activities offer fun and meaningful ways for students to become part of a positive classroom community—caring for one another and developing into socially-responsible individuals.

Why Is Classroom Community Important?

A sense of community was, at one time, more a part of life in our society. Out of necessity, people would come together to help one another. Caring and sharing were natural components of daily life. However, in today's society, these traits are sometimes replaced by individualism and competition.

Today's children witness violence on television, in the movies, and, more tragically, in their neighborhoods and homes. Many are victims of abuse and neglect. As a result, too many children are not a part of a caring community in their daily lives.

As our students grow up, they will face a very competitive job market. Our society has moved from the Industrial Age into the Information Age. Workers are required to possess critical thinking skills as well as skills in cooperation and collaboration. The structure of the workplace, in addition to a changing population, requires workers to cooperate with one another, understanding and respecting diverse groups of people.

For many children, a safe, happy, caring classroom environment is the starting point toward a bright future. As students learn to care and develop positive character traits, they experience success both academically and socially. Success breeds success. Forming happy, socially-responsible children should be the goal of every parent and teacher. Our future depends on it.

What Does a Classroom Community Look Like?

As members of this community, students really know one another. They feel they belong. Students know they are cared for and are expected to care for others. Each day, students share the responsibility for achieving common goals.

Respect is highlighted and demonstrated in a caring classroom community. Students are concerned about everyone's welfare. They encourage one another. Students are involved in making important decisions that affect the classroom community.

Teachers have clear expectations for student work and behavior. Teachers and students view mistakes as a natural part of the learning process and not as a sign of failure. Students are viewed as responsible learners and are treated equitably. They collaborate on schoolwork for better understanding.

Students celebrate the diversity of individual skills and talents brought to their classroom. They feel the support and security that comes from being part of a close-knit group. At the same time, students retain their individuality, feeling free to differ from one another.

What Are the Rights of Learners in a Classroom Community?

All members of a community have certain rights. A classroom community is no different. To ensure positive growth both academically and socially, keep in mind 12 basic rights students have in a caring classroom community. Children in a caring classroom community have a right to . . .

- be personally greeted and welcomed into the classroom each day.
- be challenged by a rigorous curriculum that helps them develop to their full potential.
- frequently cooperate and collaborate with their peers.
- socialize with their friends.
- choose learning activities.
- enjoy themselves each day.
- make mistakes without receiving criticism.
- be respected by their peers and teacher.
- be involved in critical decisions that affect their classroom community.
- talk and listen to one another.
- ask for assistance when needed and receive that assistance.
- be safe physically and emotionally.

When teachers work to protect these basic rights, a caring, socially-responsible community of learners results.

Through the implementation of character-building definitions, posters, and activities, your students will become teammates, learning partners, and best of all, trusted friends. Each character-building section begins with a definition of the character trait, a list of practical applications of that trait, and a poster idea. Enlarge, decorate, and display the posters to remind students of their character-building efforts.

Consider one of the following models as you plan to incorporate character- and community-building activities into your curriculum.

Character Trait of the Month

Devote one full month to the development of a specific character trait such as respect, compassion, kindness, friendship, self-discipline, perseverance, honesty, trust, or responsibility. Center activities and discussion around the character trait, integrating it into the curriculum.

The "T.V. Commercial" Method

Use activities from a variety of chapters (like short commercials that appeal to short attention spans), concentrating on several character traits at a time. After each activity, explain or have students guess which character traits were the focus of the activity.

Pick and Choose

After observing your students the first month of school, determine which character traits they need to develop most. Concentrate on those traits first, teaching other character traits after your students have made progress.

School-Wide Program

Choose a character trait to highlight for one week. Invite all staff, including physical education, music, and art teachers to use activities from a chapter. Ask the principal to hold a character-trait assembly in which classes perform skits, give presentations, or relay special announcements. Have every class make and hang posters highlighting the character trait. Have grade-level teachers meet and choose activities to complete simultaneously.

After you have decided how to structure your character-building program, use the activity ideas presented in this book as a first step toward establishing a cohesive unit of students working together toward a common goal.

Goals for a Happy Classroom

Instead of posting rules, invite students to brainstorm their own goals for a happy classroom. Before the class brainstorming session, establish "ground rules" such as *Goals should promote a positive and healthy learning environment; Goals should begin with a positive action word;* and *Teachers and students should work toward the goals.* Goals could include *Try your best at work and play; Listen carefully; Pick up after yourself; Take turns; Share; Help others;* and *Say* please *and* thank you. Write each goal on a separate piece of posterboard. Divide students into groups. Distribute a goal poster and crayons or markers to each group. Invite each group to illustrate the goal on their poster. Display the posters all year. (When students generate their own goals, they feel their ideas and comments are valued and are more apt to follow them.)

Naming the Class

As a class, brainstorm group identities such as the Chicago Bears, University of Kentucky Wildcats, or Greenpeace. Discuss the desire to establish a common identity for your class, emphasizing that the group name should be positive. (Miller's Meanies would not be acceptable.) Provide a few examples to get students thinking, such as a play on your last name (General's Soldiers or Street's Lights) or an alliteration (Mangan's Moonbeams). If your name is difficult to work with, use your room number to generate a name (Room 108 Greats). Place students in small groups to brainstorm possible names. Bring the class back together and compile a list of suggestions. Discuss the suggestions and decide upon one name. Use the name routinely when referring to the class (e.g., *Good morning, Moonbeams!*). Using the name, develop a few cheers or chants for test preparation and other times when motivation is needed.

Class T-Shirt

MATERIALS

students' favorite T-shirts

drawing paper

crayons, markers

plain T-shirts

fabric paints

Hold a Community T-Shirt Day, asking students to wear favorite T-shirts that advertise a community or organization. For example, students might wear a shirt depicting their favorite sports team, university, church, school, or summer camp. (Be sure to wear one, too!) Have a T-shirt fashion show, allowing each student to model and discuss his or her T-shirt. Compare the shirts and discuss their common elements. Divide students into small groups and ask them to design a T-shirt for their classroom community. Invite groups to share their designs and discuss positive aspects of each shirt. Have the class choose a favorite element from each group and combine them into one design. Invite students to duplicate the design on blank T-shirts using fabric paint. Agree upon a day for all classroom community members to wear their shirts, such as every Friday or the last Friday of the month. Students can also wear their shirts on field trips and during special events and assemblies.

Neat Sheet

MATERIALS

twin bedsheet

markers, fabric paint

Use a "neat sheet" to develop class pride and identity. In large print, write your class name, grade level, room number, and school year in the middle of a bedsheet. Divide the class into groups. Have each group decorate a section of the sheet using markers or fabric paint. Use the decorated sheet throughout the year as a Parent's Night or Open House tablecloth, class presentation backdrop, and class pride bulletin board.

MATERIALS

stuffed animal or puppet

tote bag

blank journal

Class Mascot and Journal

Bring in a stuffed animal, puppet, or other object that characterizes the class name. Place the mascot and a blank journal in a tote bag. Tell students they will have an opportunity to take the mascot home and write about their experiences with it. (For younger students, ask parents to take dictation.) To model, take the mascot home first. Write a rich, detailed, humorous story chronicling your experiences together. Share the story with the class. Invite each child to take the mascot and journal home. Be sure to provide plenty of time for students to read their stories aloud.

MATERIALS

flags or flag pictures

art supplies (colored construction paper, crayons, colored pencils, markers, paint, glue)

colored felt

Class Flag

Display flags from countries, states, and corporations. Discuss the symbolism associated with each flag. Ask each student to use art supplies and design a flag for the classroom community. Display students' work and discuss each flag's elements. Divide the class into groups of four to design another flag. Have groups incorporate elements from individual student flags. Display the new flags and, as a community, vote to choose a flag to symbolize the classroom community. Invite volunteers to duplicate that flag using felt and glue. Display the new flag in the classroom. Invite a student volunteer to carry the flag at school functions such as assemblies and Track and Field Day. An excellent time to complete this activity is United Nations Day, October 24.

Friendship Circle

MATERIALS

yarn or Koosh ball

Divide a section of chalkboard into four columns. Label the first column *Sharing,* the second *Compliments* (writing *I thank . . . , I commend . . . , I appreciate . . . ,* and *I applaud . . .* underneath), the third *Solutions,* and the fourth *Funnies.* Throughout the week, have volunteers sign up under a column so they can speak during Friendship Circle that week. (Students should sign up under one column only.)

Those who sign up for Sharing share anything they want to communicate to the rest of the class. Students who sign up for Compliments give specific praise to a classmate. Students who sign up for Solutions have tried to solve a problem and cannot resolve it. Students share the problem so the rest of the class can offer advice. Students who sign up for Funnies tell jokes, riddles, or puns.

Conduct Friendship Circle at the same time each week. Have students sit in a circle (joining hands, if you wish). Appoint a leader to begin singing a friendship song or read a poem as the official opening. Have the leader pass the yarn or Koosh ball to the first person who signed up for Sharing. After Sharing students have spoken, the ball is passed to the first person who signed up for Compliments. When the ball has been passed to everyone who wants to give compliments, it is passed to the first person who signed up for Solutions. When all solutions have been discussed, Friendship Circle ends on an upbeat note with Funnies.

MATERIALS

Closing Circle

Complete this activity approximately ten minutes before dismissal. Each day, ask a different question, inviting each student to respond. (Allow students to pass if they do not wish to share.) For example, on Monday, ask students to share a highlight from their weekend. On Tuesday, ask students a hypothetical question such as *What would be the first thing you would do if you suddenly won a million dollars?* On Wednesday, ask students to evaluate an element of the class about which you need feedback, such as *What part of adding gives you the most trouble?* On Thursday, ask students to share their favorite lesson from the week. On Friday, name a Student of the Week (for the following week) and ask each member of the class to share one thing they like about him or her.

MATERIALS

chart paper

markers

Getting to Know You

Complete this activity at the beginning of the year. On chart paper, write interview questions such as *What is your name? How old are you? Where were you born? What is one thing you want everyone to know about you? Whom do you admire? What is your favorite pastime?* or *What do you like most about school?* Have students find partners. Ask each student to take ten minutes to interview his or her partner, finding out information from the list and asking any additional questions he or she wishes. Have the class form a large circle. Invite partners to share what they learned about each other.

Respect

showing others consideration, admiration, and honor

Poster Idea

Enlarge, decorate, and display the following poster to remind students to show respect.

A classroom of respectful children—a wonderful thought—and for many teachers, a wonderful reality. In school, children with respect

- listen.
- keep unkind thoughts to themselves.
- speak kindly to teachers and other students.
- play fairly.
- wait their turn.
- raise their hand before talking.
- say *please* and *thank you*.
- clean up after themselves.
- share.
- have respect for themselves as well as others.

I Love English! ABC Book

Read aloud *I Hate English!,* the story of a Chinese girl who moves to the United States and struggles with the English language. Discuss the difficulties a person has when coming to a new country and learning its language. Have students pretend the story's main character is in their class. Assign a letter of the alphabet to each student. Ask him or her to think of a word beginning with that letter that would be important for the character to know. Write each student's word on a separate piece of construction paper. Have students illustrate their words and bind them into a class book designed to help the character with English. Entitle the book *I Love English!* As an extension, offer the book as a welcome gift for a new student who is learning English. If the new student arrives after a first book is made, have students make another book dealing with a currently-taught subject such as the farm, the ocean, or community helpers.

MATERIALS

Scarecrow reproducible (page 13)

art supplies (construction paper, yarn, string, feathers, straws, buttons)

crayons, markers

scissors

brass fasteners

If I Only Had Respect

Discuss *The Wizard of Oz* and how the scarecrow wanted a brain and felt he could get respect from others if he had one. Have students brainstorm ways people can earn others' respect, such as taking care of their appearance, speaking in a kind manner, being polite, and doing their best. Write student suggestions on the chalkboard. Distribute a scarecrow reproducible to each student. Invite students to choose three favorite suggestions from the chalkboard (or create new ideas) and write them inside the scarecrow's patches. Invite students to decorate the scarecrows with art supplies, cut them out, and connect the arms and legs with brass fasteners. Display the scarecrows on a bulletin board entitled *If I Only Had Respect.*

Scarecrow

MATERIALS

glass bowl

cold water

blue food coloring

one quart (one liter) bleach

measuring spoons

Chase the Blues Away

Have students form a circle around a table holding a glass bowl three-fourths full of cold water, container of blue food coloring, and quart (liter) of bleach. Tell students the water represents feelings. Ask volunteers to describe a time when they were treated disrespectfully. After each story, add a drop of blue food coloring to the water. Have students describe what they see. Discuss the meaning of the phrase *feeling blue*, and name feelings associated with blue. Invite volunteers to describe a time when they were treated with respect. After each story, add approximately two to three tablespoons (30 to 45 ml) of bleach to the water. Ask students to describe what they see (the water begins to turn yellow). Have students name feelings associated with yellow. Remind students that people feel sunny, bright, and happy like the color yellow when treated with respect. To close, have students write about or draw pictures of their favorite thing to do to chase the blues away. (Safety note: Remind students they should not drink water after bleach is added.)

MATERIALS

recipes brought in by students

ethnic cookbooks

foods prepared by students

bookbinding materials

Melting-Pot Cookbook

Discuss cultural diversity and the need for respect for people of all cultures. Have each student interview family members to discover his or her cultural heritage. As part of the interview, ask students to write the name of one country from which their ancestors came and one family recipe from that country. (Help students find a recipe in a cookbook if their family does not know one.) On a designated day, have students bring in foods made from their recipes for a diversity luncheon. Have each student introduce the food by telling its name and country of origin. After the luncheon, compile the recipes to make a Melting-Pot Cookbook. Distribute a cookbook to each student. (If you wish, have students sell the cookbooks to earn money for admission to an upcoming multicultural event.)

Saying *Good-Bye* to Put-Downs

MATERIALS

paper slips

gray construction paper

crayons, markers

shoe box

shovel

scissors

Explain that part of respecting others is using respectful language. On a paper slip, have each student write a hurtful put-down he or she never wants to hear again. Invite volunteers to share what they wrote and explain why the words hurt. Have students create construction-paper tombstones for the put-downs. Ask students to place the put-downs in a shoe box. Bury the put-down box outside during a class funeral ceremony. Display the tombstones in the classroom, and discuss what students can do to keep the put-downs from coming back. Implement one or two suggestions, and post reminders.

Special Student Suitcase

MATERIALS

Ira Sleeps Over by Bernard Waber

chart paper

small suitcase

marker

Label a small suitcase *S.S.S.* and set it aside. Read *Ira Sleeps Over* aloud. Discuss Ira's embarrassment and shyness regarding the sleep-over and his need for a teddy bear. Have students brainstorm ways they could show Ira respect when he revealed the teddy bear. Record the suggestions on chart paper and display. Reveal the suitcase, explaining that *S.S.S.* stands for *Special Student Suitcase*. Tell the class that each student will have a chance to be like Ira and bring an item from home that makes him or her feel special. Each night, send the suitcase home with a different student to place a special item inside. (You may wish to tape parent directions with a list of suggested items inside the suitcase. Items could include a photograph, favorite book, souvenir, award or trophy, or club or team uniform.) During each student's sharing time, remind students of the "respect suggestions" displayed on the chart. Have the student with the suitcase unpack it and share his or her special item with the class.

MATERIALS

books about the rain forest such as
The Great Kapok Tree
by Lynne Cherry

Journey of the Red-Eyed Tree Frog
by Tanis Jordan

Rain Forest
by Helen Cowcher

Here Is the Tropical Rain Forest
by Madeleine Dunphy

We Need Rain Forests reproducible
(page 17)

Respecting Nature

Read aloud and discuss several books about rain forests. Discuss the interdependence between people and nature, and the respect we should show the earth. Explain the need to maintain rain forests (for oxygen and the food they provide) rather than deplete them for unnecessary products, cattle grazing, and lumber. Distribute We Need Rain Forests reproducibles. For each item made from a rain-forest product, have students think of a real or imaginary substitute and write it in the right column. Throughout the year, remind students to conserve items made from rain-forest plants, such as erasers, rubber bands, aluminum, and hand lotion.

MATERIALS

portrait-making supplies (construction paper, chalk, paint, paintbrushes, crayons, markers)

books about grandparents such as
Anna, Grandpa, and the Big Storm
by Margot Tomes

Happy Birthday, Grampie
by Ronald Himler

Song and Dance Man
by Karen Ackerman

The Wednesday Surprise
by Eve Bunting

Knots on a Counting Rope
by Bill Martin, Jr. and John Archambault

Wilfred Gordon McDonald Partridge
by Mem Fox

writing paper

Grandparents' Day

Discuss the concept of respect as it relates to older generations. Invite students to draw portraits of a special grandparent or older friend. Have each student share the portrait and a favorite story about that person. Read aloud a variety of grandparent books. Discuss student reactions to the stories. Invite students to write "I love you" letters to their grandparents or older friends, inviting them to school on a designated day. On the special day, have students share their stories and portraits, and invite grandparents and older friends to share favorite "grandchild stories." Engage the class and their visitors in special art projects, sing-alongs, and games.

We Need Rain Forests

Name _____

Rain-Forest Plant	Product Made from Plant	Real or Imaginary Substitute
1. chicle	chewing gum	
2. bay rum	hand lotion	
3. camphor	insect repellent, medicine	
4. coconut	lotions, soaps	
5. lime	soap, bath oil	
6. patchouli	perfume, soap	
7. rubber	balloons	
8. rubber	erasers	
9. rubber	hoses	
10. rubber	rubber bands	
11. rubber	rubber gloves	
12. rubber	tires	
13. jute	rope, twine	
14. balsa	model airplanes	

MATERIALS

8" (20 cm) paper squares

crayons, markers

laminating machine

hole punch

colored yarn

expandable curtain rod

Respect Quilt

Provide each student with a paper square. Invite students to think of someone they personally know for whom they have great respect. On the paper's front, have each student draw a picture of the person, and on the back, write why he or she respects that person. Laminate each square and punch a hole in each corner. Using colored yarn, weave the squares together into rows to make a "quilt." Hang the quilt from an expandable curtain rod under the title *A Quilt of Many Heroes*.

What's Your Sign?

Explain that people around the world communicate in different languages. Ask students how they can show respect to people who speak another language. Explain that one way to show respect is to try to learn a new language. Tell students they will learn a new, very special language. Discuss sign language and why it is used. Read *The Handmade Alphabet* aloud. Using the book, teach students how to sign each letter of the alphabet. Throughout the year, invite students to sign their names and simple words. For extra fun, sign students' initials or first names as a signal for lining up or going back to their seats. Extend the activity by teaching signs for positive phrases such as *I love you* and *Good morning*.

Positive Attitude

keeping an accepting, content outlook

Poster Idea

Enlarge, decorate, and display the following poster to remind students to keep a positive attitude.

Part of learning is facing challenges and making mistakes. Children should learn to expect mistakes and challenges. These situations are easier to accept when children maintain a positive attitude. In a classroom setting, children with a positive attitude

- focus on the good rather than the bad.
- use positive language to make a point.
- naturally give compliments.
- understand it is okay to make mistakes and try to correct them.
- have dreams for the future and believe they can come true.
- show appreciation for others' efforts.
- give their best effort in every endeavor.
- trust in themselves, their teachers, and their classmates.
- accept diversity in others without trying to change them.

MATERIALS

the poem "I Have Something in My Pocket" by Harriet F. Heywood

Adapted from the *Brownie Smile Song. Brownie Smile Song* words and music by Harriet Heywood, by permission of the Girl Scouts of the United States of America.

I Have Something in My Pocket, Part One

Teach the following poem to the class. Invite students to recite the poem before performances, class photos, or anytime they need positive attitudes and gigantic grins.

I have something in my pocket; it belongs across my face.
And I keep it very close at hand in a most convenient place.
I know you couldn't guess it if you guess a long, long while.
So I'll take it out and put it on, it's a great big (your grade) smile.

MATERIALS

construction paper

crayons, markers

scissors

Pocket reproducible
(page 21)

glue

bookbinding materials

I Have Something in My Pocket, Part Two

After teaching the above poem "I Have Something in My Pocket," invite students to share items, besides smiles, that help people maintain a positive attitude. Invite students to use construction paper and crayons or markers to draw one of the suggestions. Have each student cut out the item and set it aside. Distribute a pocket reproducible to each student. Have each student decorate the pocket and glue the edges to construction paper, leaving the top edge of the pocket unglued. Invite each student to place the positive-attitude item inside the designed pocket and write the item's name underneath. Collect the pockets and bind them into a class book entitled *I Have Something in My Pocket—a Positive Attitude!*

Pocket

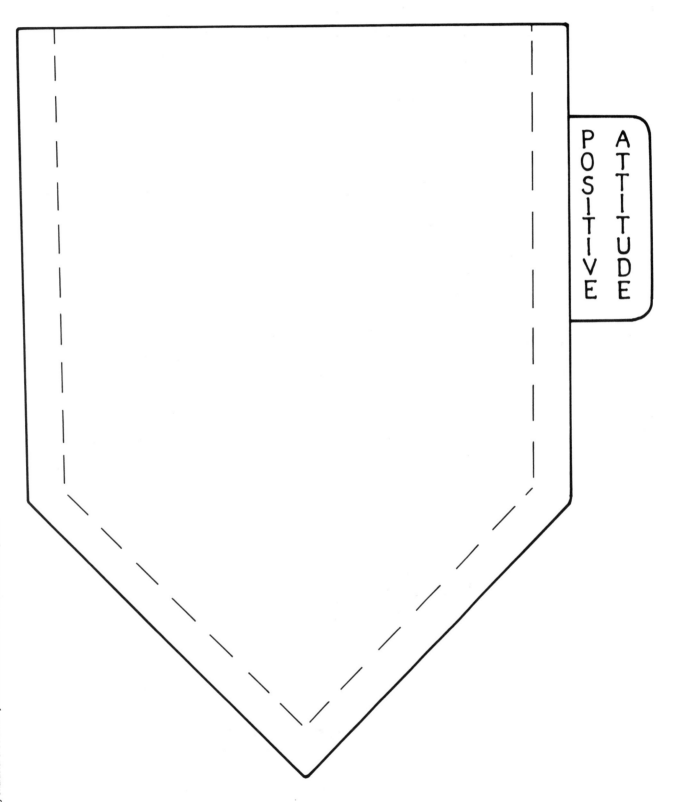

POSITIVE ATTITUDE

The Glass Is Half Full!

Show the class a glass half full of water. Recite the phrase, *Some people see the glass half full, others see it half empty.* Discuss the phrase's meaning, the most positive way to view the glass, and how the phrase can apply to a positive attitude in everyday life. Discuss how a person's attitude can affect how he or she views the world. To help students keep a "glass is half full" attitude, invite them to make their own positive-attitude glasses. Distribute a large plastic cup to each student. Invite students to use fabric paint or permanent markers to decorate their cups with positive-attitude symbols such as smiles, happy faces, or "thumbs-up" hands. Have students use their glasses as pencil holders and daily reminders to keep a positive attitude.

Top Banana

Reproduce and cut out several Top Banana badges. Each morning, choose one child to be "Top Banana." Hide a plastic banana in his or her desk to be found when students arrive. Present a badge to the Top Banana. The Top Banana not only becomes that day's messenger, line leader, and teacher's helper, he or she becomes the positive-attitude maker—the person in charge of encouraging anyone who is feeling sad, discouraged, or frustrated.

The Number Right

MATERIALS

stapler

Instead of writing the number students answer incorrectly when marking papers, write the number students answer correctly. If a student answers none correctly, write *Oops!* or *Try Again!* on the paper, and staple a new paper to the back of the first. (That way students immediately know they have a second chance.) With these practices, both you and your students will have a more positive attitude.

A Pat on the Back

MATERIALS

markers

butcher paper

scissors

art supplies
(crayons, markers, paint, paintbrushes)

hand patterns

glue

Have students find partners. Distribute butcher paper and markers to each student. Have partners lie on the floor and trace each other's outlines to form silhouettes. Ask students to cut out their silhouettes and decorate them to show their backs (back of head and clothing). Distribute a hand pattern to each student. Have each student write five things he or she can do well, one on each finger of the hand. Ask students to glue the hands to their silhouettes. Display the silhouettes on a wall under the heading *Give Yourself a Pat on the Back!*

MATERIALS

Keep up the Good Work!

When sharing stories or artwork, have the author/artist select three classmates to compliment his or her work to help keep a positive attitude. Teach students to open their compliments with *I like the way you ____ because ____. Keep up the good work!*

MATERIALS

Smiling Sessions

To put students in a good mood while working and help them maintain a positive attitude, try this fun, easy activity. At an unexpected moment, have students freeze and stop whatever they are doing. Ask students to smile as big as they can for 30 seconds. In just a few seconds, the entire class will be giggling. As a variation, challenge students not to smile and hold a "straight face." Within seconds, giggles will break out all over. When 30 seconds pass, ask students to calmly return to their work.

Amazing Grace

Read *Amazing Grace* aloud. Ask students to describe Grace's personality and how her positive attitude helped her secure the role of Peter Pan. Ask students to imagine they are Grace and think of one thing they could do to maintain a positive attitude and get "psyched up" for play tryouts. Invite each student to share his or her suggestion. Write the suggestions on chart paper. Throughout the year, review the suggestions whenever students face challenges or new learning ventures.

> ## How to Keep a Positive Attitude
>
> - I picture myself doing well.
> - I practice <u>a lot</u>.
> - I ask for help from a friend.
> - I tell myself a joke.

Be Who You Want to Be

Teach the poem/song "Free to Be You and Me." Discuss its meaning, and invite students to think about what they want to become when they grow up. Form a circle. Invite students to share what they want to become and one thing they can do to make it happen. Go around the circle two more times, inviting students to use their imaginations and think of other things they want to be. To close, remind students that they have control over their future, and that much of their future depends on their attitude.

Stretch Breaks

To help students maintain a positive attitude during concentrated or challenging work, invite them to take a stretch break. At an unexpected moment, have students freeze and stop whatever they are doing. Ask students to stand up. Lead stretches and silent exercises for one minute, inviting students to stretch high and low, run silently in place, twist, and do arm circles. After students have "loosened up," have them resume work.

"I Can" Cans

Discuss the concept of keeping a positive attitude by acknowledging oneself for accomplishments. Explain that we should be proud of what we can do and remember our good qualities when we are feeling down. Distribute a can to each student. Invite him or her to cover the can with construction paper and use art supplies to decorate it. Have students write their names on the cans and write one thing they are proud they can do. Display the cans by stacking them in a pyramid under the heading *See What We Can Do!*

Two for One

MATERIALS

Whenever a student is caught criticizing a classmate, have the criticizing student give the classmate two compliments for every criticism he or she made. Students will have a great time "catching each other." Making a game of it takes the sting out of insensitive remarks. Best of all, students quickly learn to be positive when speaking with classmates.

Positive Attitude Soup

MATERIALS

Mean Soup by Betsy Everitt

construction paper

scissors

crayons, markers

black plastic pot

wooden spoon

Ask students to name favorite soups and describe the ingredients. Display the cover of *Mean Soup.* Ask students to predict the ingredients in mean soup. Read the book aloud. After story discussion, distribute construction paper, scissors, and crayons or markers. Ask each student to use the materials to create one ingredient for Positive Attitude Soup. Gather the class around a black plastic pot. Invite each student to describe his or her ingredient and drop it in the pot. Stir the pot with a wooden spoon after each ingredient is added while the class chants, *When your head has started to droop, eat some Positive Attitude Soup!*

Happy Faces = PMA All Day!

Give a paper circle to each student when he or she enters the classroom. Explain the meaning of *PMA*—Positive Mental Attitude. Recite and explain the phrase, *Happy Faces = PMA All Day*. Have each student draw a face on the circle as a reminder to maintain a positive learning attitude all day long. Encourage students to add messages or titles to their faces. Tape the faces inside desks, cubbies, or lockers to remind students to keep a positive mental attitude.

Happy All the Time

Teach the following chant and accompanying actions to encourage students to maintain positive attitudes. Have students perform the chant before tests, performances, presentations, or competitive games.

I'm in right, out right, up right, down right, happy all the time.
(four claps)
I'm in right, out right, up right, down right, happy all the time.
(four claps)
I'm in right, out right, up right, down right, happy all the time.
(four claps)

Conflict Resolution/ Problem Solving

finding solutions in a fair, peaceful manner

Poster Idea

Enlarge, decorate, and display the following poster to help students solve problems peacefully.

One sign of maturity and character development is the ability to peacefully resolve conflicts. When children solve their own problems, a teacher can put the referee's whistle aside and provide quality education. When a problem-solving classroom environment is established, children

- compromise when necessary.
- follow teachers' or leaders' directions without complaint.
- resolve conflicts through peaceful discussion.
- work for the common good.
- treat others fairly.
- use kind rather than unkind language.
- accept change.
- openly accept differences of opinion.
- think of others—put themselves "in other people's shoes."

MATERIALS

index cards

hat

Sticky Situations

Write ten "sticky situations"—situations that could cause conflict or problems— on individual index cards. (For example, *A child in a wheelchair wants to join in a game of basketball. What should you do?; A new boy comes to class. He looks and dresses differently and speaks another language. How should you treat the new student?; or A classmate took your hat. Your name was not in it and she says it is hers. What should you do?*) Divide the class into five groups. Ask students from each group to choose two cards from a hat. Help each group read their cards and plan a short role play showing a solution for each. Invite each group to practice and perform for the class. After each role play, discuss if the sticky situation was handled appropriately. Brainstorm other solutions if necessary.

MATERIALS

shoe box

crayons, markers

scissors

paper slips

Suggestion Box

Decorate a shoe box, cut a slit in the lid, and write *Suggestion Box* on the front. Once a week, invite a volunteer to share a problem he or she has been having at school. The problem could be with a school subject, another student, or any situation. Distribute a paper slip to each student. Ask students to draw or write possible solutions to the volunteer's problem, write their names on the slips, and place them in the suggestion box. Have the volunteer shake the box and choose five slips. When the volunteer calls the name on a slip, have that student stand and share his or her solution. After the slips are shared, ask the volunteer to choose two solutions he or she likes best and keep the slips as a reminder to try them.

Substitute Solutions

MATERIALS

Miss Nelson Is Missing by Harry Allard

chart paper

Read *Miss Nelson Is Missing* aloud. After discussing the story, display a piece of chart paper. On the left side, write the heading, *Problem!* On the right side, write the heading, *Instead . . . .* As a class, have students recall examples of misbehavior by students in the story. Write each example under *Problem!* For each misbehavior, have students think of one thing story characters could have done instead to make their teacher feel respected and loved. Write these examples under *Instead . . . ,* next to their corresponding problems. Relate the chart to behavior with a substitute teacher in your class. Keep the chart. The night before having a substitute teacher, display the chart in a prominent place under the heading, *Remember Miss Nelson!*

Invention Convention

MATERIALS

items from home

display tables

Explain that inventions are often made because a person has a problem and needs to solve it. Discuss everyday problems such as babies crying, shoelaces coming untied, jars not opening, and paper cuts. Invite each student to share a problem he or she wishes had a better solution. Ask each student to choose one suggestion for which to create an original invention. Send a letter home to parents explaining the assignment and inviting their entire family to participate. Have families work on their inventions for three to four weeks. Then, hold an Invention Convention in a large room with display tables. Have students and their families display their inventions, tell the problems the inventions solve, and explain the solutions. Invite other classes to attend.

I Want It!

Read *I Want It!* aloud. Just before the story's conflict is resolved, stop reading. Invite students to brainstorm ways to solve the problem and predict the story's resolution. Finish reading the book. After story discussion, invite each student to replace the original story resolution with his or her own problem-solving technique. Have each student illustrate the new technique on drawing paper. Ask students to write an explanation for their illustrations at the bottom of the pages. Collect the illustrations and bind them in a class book entitled *Better Ways to Get What You Want!*

Flying High

Discuss common problems that cause upset feelings and blaming in class. Discuss positive ways to solve these problems such as sharing, taking turns, using respectful language, compromising, and listening. List problem-solving techniques on large kite-shaped butcher paper. Hang the butcher-paper kite in the center of a large bulletin board entitled *These Kids Are Flying High!* Have each student use construction paper to draw and cut out a self-portrait, and staple it to the bulletin board. Whenever you catch a student using a problem-solving technique from the kite, give him or her a diamond-shaped cutout. Have the student decorate the diamond to resemble a kite, attach a piece of string, and hang it on the bulletin board so his or her self-portrait is "flying" it. Invite students to add a bow-tie cutout (kite ribbon) to their kites each time you "catch them" being good.

Role Reversal

MATERIALS

Whenever a conflict arises between two students, have them trade places and explain the incident through the other person's point of view. Teach students to use *I feel ____ when ____* statements as they explain. For example, a student who pushed another might say, *I felt hurt and scared when you pushed me.* The pushed student might say, *I felt bad when you called me a name so I pushed you.* After the role reversal, discuss the situation and ways to avoid problems in the future.

Finish This

MATERIALS

construction paper

crayons, markers

Challenge students to use problem-solving skills with this fun indoor-recess activity. Divide the class into pairs. Distribute a piece of construction paper and crayons or markers to each pair. Tell pairs they are going to draw a story together but they cannot talk to each other. Have one partner start by drawing an object such as an airplane, flower, person, or house. Have that student pass the paper to his or her partner. Have the partner think about the object and then add to the illustration by drawing another object that relates to the first. As the illustration becomes more complicated, students must use problem-solving skills to think of ways to connect the drawings and show a story. Have students continue drawing and trading until an entire story can be told from the illustration. Invite pairs to share their scenes. During discussion, ask questions such as *What was the hardest part of making your drawing? How did you solve problems with your partner without talking? Was there any conflict during drawing time? How did you solve it?*

MATERIALS

Me First by Dandi D. Knorr

small box

markers

pennies

dice

First by Chance

Read *Me First* aloud. After discussing the story, help students solve the "I-want-to-go-first" problem for games and group projects with a First-by-Chance Box. Decorate a box and label it *First by Chance*. Place pennies and dice inside. Whenever students have to choose a first player, have them go to the box and flip a coin or roll the dice to determine a winner. Winners choose whether to go first or last.

MATERIALS

Heart and Hand reproducible
(page 35)

scissors

craft sticks

glue

Use Hearts, Not Hands

Explain that the best way to settle problems is to "use hearts, not hands," settling problems through peaceful, compassionate dialogue rather than violence. Have students cut out the heart and hand on the reproducible. Ask students to glue the heart to one side of a craft stick and the hand to the other. Read aloud several school-day situations such as *Someone politely asked for crayons. What did he or she use?* or *Someone kicked you during recess. What did he or she use?* After reading each situation, invite students to hold up one side of the stick (a heart or hand) to show how the problem was handled. For "hand" situations, discuss a "hearts, not hands" way to settle the conflict.

Heart and Hand

I Need to Talk

Photocopy several "I Need to Talk" notes. Place the notes in a can labeled *Notes*. Place an empty can labeled *I Need to Talk* next to the *Notes* can. Whenever students have a problem they want to discuss privately, have them take a note from the *Notes* can, write their name on it, and place it in the *I Need to Talk* can. Every other day, empty the can and meet with students privately to discuss their problems.

Name:_____

Date:_____

I need to talk.

Name:_____

Date:_____

I need to talk.

Name:_____

Date:_____

I need to talk.

Name:_____

Date:_____

I need to talk.

Self-Discipline

controlling one's own thoughts and behavior

Poster Idea

Enlarge, decorate, and display the following poster to remind students to exercise self-discipline.

Don't Be Distracted—Stay on Track!

When children demonstrate self-discipline in the classroom, they make learning easier for themselves and others. A large part of becoming self-disciplined is understanding why it is important. After children understand the importance of self-discipline, they need to learn how to exercise it.

Children who exercise self-discipline in the classroom

- complete their assignments.
- stay on task.
- wait to be called on.
- work toward personal and community goals.
- try again and again.
- ignore peer pressure.
- choose productive rather than destructive activities.
- control their tempers.

I Have Ten Little Fingers

To help students focus their attention, get ready to listen, and set the stage for self-discipline, teach the following finger play.

I have ten little fingers and they all belong to me.

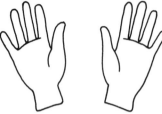

I can make them do things. Would you like to see?

I can shut them tight. I can open them wide.

I can put them together. I can make them hide.

I can make them wave high. I can make them wave low.

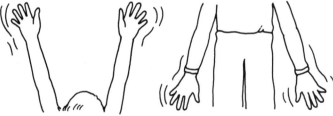

I can fold them quietly and hold them just so.

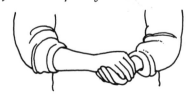

Class Chart

MATERIALS

graph or butcher paper

tape

crayons, stickers, or rubber stamps

Reward the class for practicing self-discipline by using a class chart. Invite the class to select a reward to work toward, such as a popcorn party or extra recess. Draw a large graph, or tape several pieces of graph paper together to make a chart. Hang the chart in a highly visible place. Each time you observe a student, a small group, or the whole class practicing self-discipline, invite a student to fill a chart square by coloring it, placing a sticker on it, or using a rubber stamp. When the chart is filled, treat the whole class!

Rude Rex

MATERIALS

hat and jacket

bubble gum

Have students sit on the floor in a large circle. Leave the room briefly and reenter wearing a hat and jacket and chewing gum. Come in using loud, rude behavior and displaying bad manners. Stand in the middle of the circle. Tell the class you are a new student named *Rude Rex.* Ask a student to introduce him- or herself. Demonstrate rude behavior and bad listening skills (such as looking away, blowing bubbles, interrupting, and talking to other students) as he or she speaks. Leave the room and reenter as yourself. Ask the class if anything happened while you were gone. During discussion, explain self-discipline and good listening skills. Explain the five steps to good listening when sitting in a circle: Legs are folded like a pretzel. Hands are folded in the lap. Ears are open. Lips are closed. Eyes are on the speaker. Throughout the year, remind students to practice the five steps by saying *five* or holding up five fingers.

I Can Do It!

Discuss heroes who maintained self-discipline despite others' doubts, such as Thomas Edison and Wilbur and Orville Wright. Talk about the self-discipline—time, dedication, hard work, and "thick skin"—required for these heroes to make their dreams come true. Invite students to think about one of their own dreams and the benefits of maintaining self-discipline to obtain it. Distribute I Can Do It! reproducibles and crayons or markers. Help students complete the reproducible by drawing illustrations in the boxes and writing in the speech bubble. Collect the papers and bind them into a class book entitled *I Can Do It!*

MATERIALS

index card

marker

hole punch

ribbon

stuffed animal

You Tried Your Best and Nothing Less!

On an index card, write *You tried your best and nothing less!* Punch a hole in the card, string it with ribbon, and tie the ribbon around a stuffed animal's neck. At the beginning of the day, explain that the stuffed animal will be given for the day to a student who shows great self-discipline in class. Observe students in the morning, and present the stuffed animal to a student who shows self-discipline. Explain why you have awarded the stuffed animal when presenting it. The next day, invite the student with the animal to observe classmates and give away the stuffed animal when he or she observes someone using self-discipline. Keep track of students who have received the stuffed animal. Remind students giving the animal away names of those who have received it so the animal is distributed fairly.

I Can Do It!

Name _____

My Dream for the Future

One Thing Someone Might Say to Stop Me from Making My Dream Come True

One Self-Disciplined Thing I Can Do to Show I Can Do It

MATERIALS

How Did I Do Today? reproducible
(page 43)

How Did I Do Today?

Discuss self-discipline as it relates to behavior in school. Invite students to name self-disciplined actions they perform in school. At the end of the day, remind students of the discussion and invite them to complete the self-discipline assessment *How Did I Do Today?* Collect the assessments. Have students complete assessments each day of the week. At the end of the week, discuss students' accomplishments and improvements in self-discipline.

MATERIALS

long yarn pieces

Invisible Shield

During independent, quiet work time, give each student a long yarn piece. Invite each student to create a large circle with the yarn and sit inside it while completing his or her work. Tell students that the yarn represents an invisible shield—no one can walk or talk through it. After quiet work time, invite students to discuss the self-discipline required to work within the invisible shield.

How Did I Do Today?

Name _____

1. I took turns.

2. I followed directions.

3. I encouraged and helped others.

4. I shared.

5. I listened.

6. I solved problems peacefully.

7. I used calm, kind words.

MATERIALS

adhesive name tags

Daily Goal

At the beginning of the day, have students form a circle. Invite each student to name one goal he or she has for the day, such as complete all work neatly, use only kind words, or raise his or her hand before speaking. Write each student's goal on an adhesive name tag. Invite students to place the name tags on their hands, shirts, or desks for the day as a reminder of the goal. At the end of the day, discuss each child's accomplishments and the self-discipline required to achieve goals.

MATERIALS

posterboard

crayons, markers

Give Me Five

Have students discuss actions that help them become successful at school. Tell them about five self-disciplined actions to ensure school success. On the chalkboard, write:

1. *Eyes Watching*
2. *Ears Listening*
3. *Hands Still*
4. *Brain Thinking*
5. *Heart Caring*

Discuss the meaning of each action. Invite groups to make posters advertising the five actions and entitle the posters *Give Me Five.* Hang the posters throughout the school. Have groups write short commercials to explain their posters. Invite groups to read their commercials over the P.A. system or travel from class to class performing them.

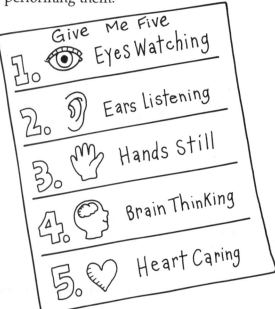

Cooperation/ Teamwork

willingly working with others toward a common goal

Poster Idea

Enlarge, decorate, and display the following poster to remind students to cooperate and work together.

In many cases, children learn best when they learn from each other. For children to work together and learn from their peers, they have to cooperate and work like a team. "Team players" are children who

- listen.
- encourage their peers.
- allow and invite others to contribute their talents and skills.
- follow as well as lead.
- recognize their strengths and use them for the common good.
- treat others equitably.
- recognize the needs of the group.
- think before acting.
- communicate calmly.
- put competition aside.

MATERIALS

Strong as Our Weakest Link

Have students form a circle and hold hands. Choose one student to lead the group through several actions (such as marching, tiptoeing, jogging, or skipping) as the rest of the class follows, without dropping hands. (Chances are, students will drop hands at least once.) After the first unsuccessful round of the game, discuss how the game relates to teamwork and cooperation. Explain that many endeavors in class will be unsuccessful if students do not work together. After a successful round, explain that when everyone works together, the whole class will be successful and strong while having fun.

MATERIALS

Clancy the Clown reproducible
(page 47)

butcher paper

tape

dice

slates

chalk

bean bags

No Clowning Around

Help students work as a team while reinforcing knowledge in content areas. Enlarge Clancy the Clown on butcher paper and tape it to the floor. Divide the class into teams of four, assigning each team a name and each team member a number. Determine the order in which teams will play by rolling dice. Begin by asking a question. Give teams 20 to 30 seconds to conference and write down an answer on a slate. Call a number between one and four to determine which team members will show the slates. Invite each team to reveal their answer. If the answer is correct, that student tosses a bean bag at Clancy to earn points. After several rounds of play, tally points to determine a winning team.

Clancy the Clown

MATERIALS

Study Buddies

Promote cooperation and teamwork among grade levels by contacting a teacher from a higher or lower grade level to set up a study-buddy program between your classes. Group each older and younger student-pair by gender, learning level, or interest area. Throughout the year, invite pairs to read and complete special projects together. Between meetings, have study buddies write notes to each other.

MATERIALS

butcher paper

crayons, markers

scissors

Partnership Puzzle

Make and display a large heart shape made from butcher paper. Draw puzzle-piece lines on the heart. Explain that the puzzle represents cooperation and teamwork in class, and each piece represents a student. Discuss how (like the puzzle and its pieces) when individuals come together and use cooperation, the whole class will get along as a "perfect fit." Cut the puzzle pieces apart, and give a piece to each student. Ask each student to draw or write one thing he or she will do to cooperate and show teamwork in school. Invite the class to put the puzzle together again. Display the partnership puzzle on a bulletin board as a daily reminder of the importance of teamwork and cooperation.

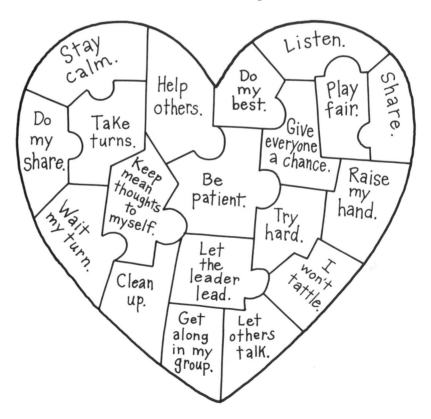

Friends Stick Together

MATERIALS

recorded music

record, cassette, or compact disc player

Have students move around the classroom to lively music. Stop the music randomly and call out, *Friends five!* (or *two, eight,* or any number smaller than the class size). Have students quickly join together to form a group with the appropriate number without making a sound or touching anyone. If the number called does not divide students evenly, have extra students stand near you in a group. After several rounds, discuss how the game takes teamwork and cooperation.

Cooperative Community

MATERIALS

tape

boxes

items from home

art supplies (butcher paper, paint, crayons, markers, glue, glitter, sequins, yarn)

Have students brainstorm ways a community's residents, businesses, and government cooperate to make the community happier and safer. For example, drivers obey traffic signs, residents place their trash near the street so trash collectors can reach it; and police patrol the streets. Invite the class to work together to create an imaginary community named *Cooperation.* Tape a large rectangular boundary on the classroom floor. Explain that the community must be built within the taped area and can be represented by buildings, mannequins, murals, music, and so on. As a class, decide if the community will be urban or rural. Have small groups use boxes, items from home, and art supplies to create examples of occupations, businesses, government buildings, and natural resources.

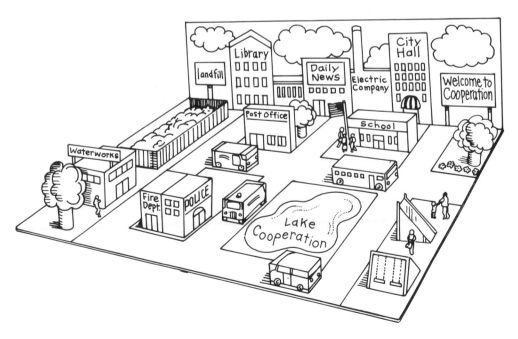

MATERIALS

Mirror, Mirror

Divide the class into pairs, and have partners face each other. Invite one partner from each pair to be the leader. Have leaders silently make movements while partners try to follow their moves exactly and simultaneously. Remind leaders that the object is to have their partners move *with* them. No tricking is allowed. Invite each pair to perform for the class. Have the class try to guess the leader. Ask partners to switch roles and repeat the activity.

MATERIALS

two large greeting cards

scissors

construction paper

crayons, markers

tape

Giant Greeting Card

Divide the class into two groups, and distribute a greeting card to each. Cut each greeting card into as many pieces as there are group members. Give each student a piece of the card, construction paper, and crayons or markers. Ask each student to draw and decorate an enlarged version of the card piece on construction paper. When finished, invite each group to piece and tape their original card together. Next, have each group piece and tape their drawings together in the same order as the original card. (The student-made cards will resemble abstract art.) Explain that the student-made cards are just like teamwork—when everyone does his or her part for the good of the group, the result is a masterpiece. Display the giant cards next to the originals.

String Game

Cut a five-foot (1.5-m) piece of yarn for every three students. Divide the class into groups of three. Tell students they will work together silently to manipulate yarn and form objects on the ground. Name several easy- and hard-to-make objects such as a triangle, star, house, or your state or country. After several rounds, have students discuss the cooperation necessary to play the game. Relate the cooperation needed in the game to that in the classroom. As an extension, play this game when studying specific subjects such as geometry (shapes), science (animal-home shapes), or grammar (punctuation marks).

MATERIALS

5' (1.5 m) yarn pieces

Seven Blind Mice

Read *Seven Blind Mice* aloud. Discuss how, individually, each mouse had difficulty determining the identity of the mystery object. Explain that when the mice worked together as a team and shared their ideas, they discovered the object was an elephant. Have volunteers name classroom tasks that would be easier if completed as a group. Chart suggestions on the chalkboard. Divide students into groups of five. Distribute gray construction paper and crayons or markers to each student. Invite one student from each group to design and cut out an elephant part—head, body, legs, ears, tail. Have each student write a different idea for a group classroom task on the elephant part. When parts are complete, invite groups to tape the elephant parts together. Display the elephants on a bulletin board surrounded by mouse cutouts.

MATERIALS

Seven Blind Mice by Ed Young

chalkboard

gray construction paper

crayons, markers

tape

mouse cutouts

What's in the Bag?

Practice teamwork and cooperation while introducing a new theme or unit by playing this game. Place an object related to the theme in a paper grocery bag and close the top. Divide students into small groups. Give groups five minutes to think of several questions. Invite groups to ask a total of 20 "yes-or-no" questions to discover what is in the bag. Have each group rotate and ask questions, reminding students to avoid repeating questions from other groups. Have a volunteer tally the number of questions asked. When the class discovers the object's identity, remove it from the bag and begin the unit.

Whisper the Message

Have students form a circle sitting on the floor. Write a secret message on a slip of paper. Start by whispering the message into the ear of the student sitting to your right. Have that student whisper the message to the person to his or her right. Have students pass the message until everyone has a turn. Invite the last student to repeat the secret message aloud. Read the message written on the paper—it will most likely be quite different from the last student's announcement! (To encourage students to listen, offer a class treat if the message is announced correctly.) Relate this activity to the open communication needed for cooperation and teamwork. Explain that, when working with a group, it is important for everyone to listen to each other and understand what other people are saying. Ask students to give examples of group situations in which all group members must listen carefully.

Partnership Walk

MATERIALS

cloth strips

Divide the class into pairs on a grassy playing field. Have partners stand one in back of the other. Have partners tie their right legs together, and then their left legs, with cloth strips. Challenge partners to work together and walk from one point to another. When students have practiced, have pairs race. Discuss the cooperation necessary to complete the game. Relate the qualities needed in the game (i.e., communication, patience, a positive attitude) to those needed for classroom activities.

Sink or Swim

MATERIALS

bulletin board supplies (letters, butcher paper, construction paper, scissors)

small plastic boat

writing paper

Create a "Sink or Swim" bulletin board, shown below, as a cooperation reminder. Discuss the board. Explain that "swimmers" are group members who listen to all ideas, keep their eyes on speakers, use quiet voices, and cooperate with votes. Explain that "sinkers" are those who are do not listen, argue, use loud voices, and "boss others around." Discuss the importance of cooperation during group work. Explain that all group members must be "swimmers" so the boat can stay afloat. During group work, observe groups for evidence of "swimmers" and "sinkers." Present a plastic boat labeled *USS Success* to a group showing cooperation. Move the boat from group to group as you notice students working well together. After group work, have each student write a reflection explaining why he or she was a "swimmer" or "sinker." To close, act as a "lifeguard" and offer advice so "sinkers" can become "swimmers." Present the boat whenever students work in groups.

Helping Out

At the beginning of the year, set up a student-helper program with the school librarian, custodian, lunch servers, and/or playground supervisors. Ask each student to choose a staff member to help and sign up for a date and time on a schedule. Over a period of weeks or months, have students work with their assigned staff members. After all students have worked with a staff member, invite volunteers to tell what they liked and disliked about the job and how they felt helping someone with their work.

Shark Attack

Take students to an open playing area, and divide them into groups of eight. Give each group a piece of cardboard just big enough for all group members to stand on. (The cardboard represents a boat.) Have each group stand at one end of the area. When you yell, *Go!*, students run forward, trying to reach the other side of the playing area. As they run, each group member must help carry the cardboard. When you yell, *Sharks!*, all group members must immediately drop the cardboard and stand on it. If one member falls off, that group must go back to the beginning and tear a chunk from their boat. After a team successfully reaches the other side of the playing area, have students discuss how cooperation was necessary to hold the cardboard, stay on the boat, and help the team. Compare the cooperation required in the game to that required in everyday living. Invite students to share times when they had to cooperate to "keep afloat."

Friendship

accepting, giving, sharing, feeling, and
enjoying companionship with others

Poster Idea

Enlarge, decorate, and display
the following poster to remind
students to be good friends.

Children naturally seek friends
like themselves. The challenge
is to help children find friendship with those different from
themselves, such as those of a
different gender, race, personal-
ity-type, stature, or academic-
or physical-ability level.
Children who become friends
with others, regardless of differences, make the classroom a
comfortable, happy place to be.
Children who are good friends

- accept others for who they are.
- share their belongings.
- listen.
- enjoy others' company.
- support others in need.
- smile, laugh, and tell jokes.
- avoid teasing and put-downs.
- encourage others with kind
  words.
- avoid tattling.
- ask for help from their peers.
- solve problems peacefully.
- consider others' feelings
  before acting.

We Learn from Our Friends

Remind students of the joy of having friends from a different culture, age group, or neighborhood with this fun activity. Read *Stellaluna* aloud. During story discussion, ask students what Stellaluna was able to learn from her bird friends and what the birds learned from her. Relate this discussion to human friendships. Invite each student to share a story of a friend who is outside his or her usual circle of companions. Distribute a bat pattern and crayons or markers to each student. On the left wing, have students draw a picture of the special friend. On the right wing, have students write the friend's name. Ask students to cut out the bats, fold the wings at the dotted lines, and attach string to the bats' backs. Hang the bats from the ceiling surrounding a suspended *Stellaluna* book cover.

Wanted: A Good Friend

As a class, brainstorm characteristics and qualities that make a good friend. Write the list on chart paper. Using an overhead projector, display and discuss newspaper "want ads" that are transferred to an overhead transparency. Tell students they will create a "want ad" for a new friend. Distribute construction paper and crayons or markers. Have younger students draw pictures of their requirements for a friend; have older students write a descriptive paragraph. Hang completed "want ads" on a bulletin board entitled *Wanted: A Good Friend!*

PHAN
Wanted: Best friend. Funny, honest, must like model airplanes. Bike rider a plus. See Phan for more information.

Bat

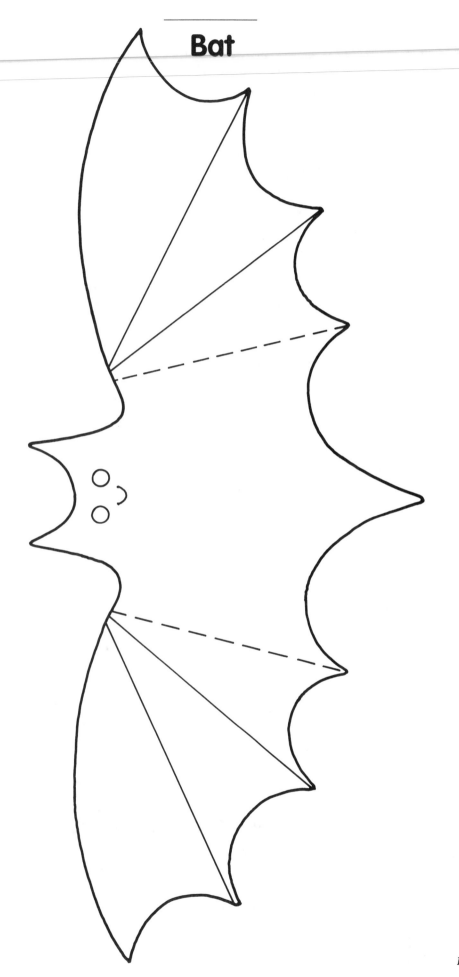

Friendship Badges

Set up a badge-making center with a laminated phrase list, blank badge reproducibles, and art supplies. Invite students to visit the center when they experience an act of friendship, choose a phrase to copy on a badge (or think of one of their own), and decorate it for the deserving friend. Have students attach double-sided tape to the badges for wearing and present them to their friends.

Cinnamon-and-Applesauce Jewelry

Discuss things friends can give, such as hugs, advice, laughter, and gifts. Tell students they will make a gift for a friend in class. Write each student's name on a paper slip, and place the slips in a paper bag. Have students choose a name from the bag. In a large bowl, combine equal amounts of applesauce and cinnamon to make modeling dough. Stir the dough until thoroughly mixed. Roll the dough on waxed paper until it is one-quarter inch (.5 cm) thick. Invite each student to press a shape in the dough with a cookie cutter and then use a straw to make a necklace hole. Have students carve compliments in the shapes with pencil tips. Allow shapes to dry overnight. Invite each student to string his or her shape onto a yarn strand and present the necklace to the person whose name he or she chose.

Phrase List

Way to go!

Best friend!

Thanks for your help!

Super job!

Keep up the good work!

I like you!

Outstanding!

Thanks!

We make a great team!

Best buddy!

You're nice!

Cool!

Badge

MATERIALS

Friendship Tag

Lead students to a large play area. Choose two students to be "it" for a game of tag. When players are tagged by the "its," they must "freeze." To become "unfrozen" and able to run again, another player must run to the "frozen" player and whisper one thing he or she likes about him or her. After three or four minutes of play, choose new students to be "it" and play again.

MATERIALS

2" x 5" (5 cm x 12.5 cm) paper strips

crayons, markers

tape

index cards

stapler

Friendship Chain

Distribute a paper strip to each student, and leave several strips on a table in the center of the room. Have each student write his or her name on the strip. Ask each student to loop and tape his or her strip to the strip of the person sitting next to him or her. Invite pairs to bring their two links to the center of the room and connect them with strips from the table and the other pairs' links to make one long chain. Hang the chain like a garland from the ceiling. Explain that the chain represents friendship—each individual link is important to the chain as a whole, just as each individual student is important to the class as a whole. Discuss times when a friendly attitude is needed by individual students so the entire class can be happy and productive. Distribute index cards and crayons or markers. Invite children to illustrate examples of friendship in class and staple their illustrations to their chain links. Create frequent opportunities for students to add new links to the friendship chain so it is constantly growing.

Friendship Box

Tape a mirror to the inside bottom of a shoe box. Replace the lid and set the box aside. Discuss qualities of a good friend, and write a list on the chalkboard. Read *The 329th Friend* aloud. After reading, ask, *What are the qualities of a good friend? How many of you are a friend to yourself?* Display the shoe box and explain that it is a Friendship Box. Pass the box from student to student and invite each to peek inside to find his or her own best friend. Ask students to remain quiet after peeking inside. After each student sees him- or herself in the mirror, have students consult the list of qualities and discuss why everyone should be his or her own best friend.

MATERIALS

shoe box

small mirror

tape

chalkboard

The 329th Friend by Marjorie Weinman Sharmat

Rainbow Fish

Read *Rainbow Fish* aloud. Discuss the importance of sharing with friends. Distribute a piece of construction paper to each student. Invite students to draw and cut out a large fish. On one side of the fish, have students draw an eye and gills and write or draw three ways they can share with a friend. On the other side, have students use art supplies to create a "rainbow fish." Have students add fins and scales made of glitter or metallic wrapping paper. Hang fish from the ceiling near a heading that reads *Sharing Hooks New Friends!*

MATERIALS

Rainbow Fish by Marcus Pfister

construction paper

art supplies (markers, paint, paintbrushes, yarn, feathers, buttons, glue)

glitter or metallic wrapping paper

string

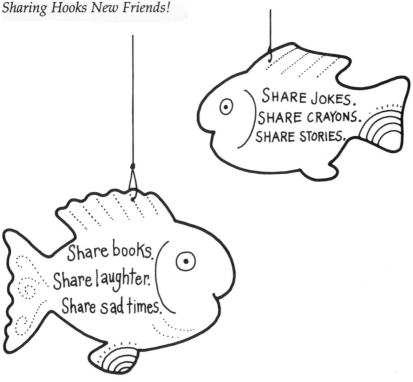

MATERIALS

tape

student photos

8 ¹/₂" x 11" (21 cm x 27.5 cm) drawing paper

stapler

Friendly Photos

Tape half the students' photos on a piece of paper, drawing a line under or next to each. Use another piece of paper and repeat with the other half. Photocopy, staple, and distribute the photo-pages. Invite students to write a positive comment about a person in a photo. Have each student trade pages with another student, choose another photo, and write a new comment. Have students trade until each line is full. Invite each student to keep the pages he or she receives last. So each student can read everything written about him- or herself, have students display pages on desks and rotate from desk to desk.

MATERIALS

tape

scissors

two large butcher-paper circles

crayons, markers

Friendship Pizza

Cut each butcher-paper circle into 16 equal triangular pieces. Give each student a triangle (a slice from a friendship pizza). Have each student write his or her name on the slice. Ask a question such as *How many brothers and sisters do you have?* Invite each student to take the pizza slice and find another person who has the same number of brothers and sisters. When students find partners, have them join their slices with tape. (If students cannot find partners, have them choose from remaining students.) Have pairs choose a representative to give an answer to a second question. Have pairs find another pair whose representative has the same answer. Ask the two pairs to join their slices to make four pieces. Ask two more questions, each time inviting student groups to choose representatives and join pizza slices with other groups until two round 16-piece pizzas are made. Hang the pizzas on a bulletin board entitled *Friendship Pizza—Each piece is great!*

Honesty/Trust

being sincere, truthful, trustworthy, and loyal

Poster Idea

Enlarge, decorate, and display the following poster to remind students to be honest and trustworthy.

Never Be Afraid to Tell the Truth! Everyone makes mistakes...

Honest is something you are. Trust is something you have. Although they are different character traits, honesty and trust are interrelated. Children trust others when they are honest. In turn, children tell the truth when they trust. In the classroom, honest, trusting children

- tell the truth despite consequences.
- voice their opinions in a kind, thoughtful way.
- "tell on" someone only when necessary.
- show and share their feelings.
- know their classmates and teacher care and want the best for them.
- feel and react without guilt.
- express themselves positively as well as critically.

MATERIALS

The Big Fat Enormous Lie by Marjorie
Weinman Sharmat

construction paper

watercolor paints

paintbrushes

What Does a Lie Look Like?

Read *The Big Fat Enormous Lie* aloud. Discuss the lie from which the boy could not hide and what a lie, if alive, might look like. Distribute paper, paint, and paintbrushes. Have students divide their papers in half. On the first half, have them paint their interpretations of a living lie. On the second half, have students paint their interpretations of the word *honesty*. Write students' descriptions under their paintings. Display paintings on a bulletin board entitled *What You See Is What You Get!*

MATERIALS

index cards

Honesty Is the Best Policy

Write several situations that require honesty on individual index cards, such as *You found a wallet with $100 in it. What might you do?* Divide students into groups of four. Have each group choose a card. Give groups five minutes to discuss their situations and choose a way to resolve them. Have each group share their situation and solution. Invite the class to decide if the solution is a good one and brainstorm other appropriate solutions.

Little White Lies

MATERIALS

Liar, Liar, Pants on Fire! by Miriam Cohen

Read *Liar, Liar, Pants on Fire!* aloud. Discuss the definition of "little white lie." Have each student think of a "little white lie" he or she has told and how the lie turned into "big bad trouble." Invite each student to share his or her little-white-lie story. After a storyteller finishes telling the little-white-lie part of his or her story, have the class chant, *Little white lie*. As they say the words, have students hold up a thumb and index finger to indicate something small. After a storyteller tells the big-bad-trouble part of the story, have the class chant, *Big bad trouble*. As they say the words, have students spread their arms out wide to indicate something large. To close, invite each student to think of ways he or she could have solved the problem without telling a little white lie.

Who Are You Going to Call?

MATERIALS

index cards

Invite volunteers to name people they trust and explain why. Have students explain why trustworthiness is important in friendship and everyday life. On the chalkboard, display the following words: *Parents, Friends, Teachers, Police.* Distribute four index cards to each student. Have students copy a word on each card. Tell students they will hear a series of "who are you going to call" problems such as *You failed a math test and need extra help. Who are you going to call?* Invite students to consider each problem and choose a group of people (from those on the cards) they would trust to help with their problem. Have students show their choices by holding up a card. Read and invite students to respond to several situations. Invite volunteers to explain why they made their choices.

MATERIALS

The Gold Coin by Alma Flor Ada

butcher paper

pastels and watercolor paints

paintbrushes

markers

round, gold paper circle

Avoid the Gold if the Truth Can't Be Told!

Read *The Gold Coin* aloud and discuss the story. Discuss Juan, and have students decide if he was being completely honest with the people he met. Ask students to explain why hiding the truth can be as dishonest as telling a lie. Have students tell what they would have done if they were Juan. Divide students into groups of three. Distribute a piece of butcher paper to each group. Ask groups to divide the butcher paper into five sections (as shown) and use paint and pastels to create a mural. Have students paint and draw in the four rectangles to show each event in the story in which Juan hid the truth. In the last section, have students use markers to write what happened, how Juan changed, and what changed him. Display the murals near a gold, coin-shaped headline stating *Avoid the Gold if the Truth Can't Be Told!*

MATERIALS

"Frog and Toad" books by Arnold Lobel

Frog and Toad reproducible (page 67)

scissors

crayons, markers

Trusted Friends Make Us Hoppy!

Use the "Frog and Toad" series for a weeklong reading unit, presenting vocabulary, reading-strategy, and comprehension activities as daily reading instruction. On the last day of the unit, ask questions about trust, such as *Could Frog and Toad always trust each other? How do you know they trusted each other?* Divide the class into pairs. Distribute a "Frog and Toad" book, a Frog and Toad reproducible, scissors, and crayons or markers to each pair. Invite pairs to review the book and find two examples of trust between Frog and Toad. Have each pair illustrate the examples, one in each character's belly on the reproducible. Invite pairs to color and cut out Frog and Toad. Display Frogs and Toads on a bulletin board entitled *Trusted Friends Make Us Hoppy!*

TOAD

FROG

Trust Rope

On the playground or in a park, string two or three tied-together clotheslines approximately three feet (one meter) off the ground, from tree to tree or object to object, to create a walking course. Be sure the path is clear of obstacles. During a trust discussion, stress the importance of trusting classmates and friends and the responsibilities of being trusted by someone. Divide the class into pairs. Have one partner from each pair put on a blindfold. Invite the blindfolded students to start at the beginning of the clotheslines course, grasp it, and follow it to the end. Ask sighted students to walk silently next to their partners, offering help only when needed. Have partners change roles and follow the clotheslines in the other direction. After the game, invite students to share how they felt during the game. Ask questions such as, *How did you feel when you were blindfolded? How did you feel knowing someone was there to help you? Did you trust your partner? Why or why not? Were you a trustworthy partner? Why or why not?*

MATERIALS

Abe Lincoln's Hat by Martha Brenner

black construction paper

scissors

glue

large coffee can

tape

writing paper

Honest Abe

In advance, make a replica of a stove-pipe hat by covering a large coffee can with black construction paper. Tape a round, black construction paper base to the can as a brim. Place the hat on a table in the center of the room. Read *Abe Lincoln's Hat* aloud. Discuss Abe's honesty, integrity, and trustworthiness as described in the story. Distribute writing paper. Have students write a paragraph or draw a picture describing a time when they were honest even though it was difficult. Ask each student to place the paper in Abe Lincoln's hat (the coffee can)—just like he did in the story! One at a time, pull the paragraphs or pictures from the hat and invite students to read or explain them to the class. After all experiences are shared, have the class applaud themselves for being like Honest Abe.

Responsibility

Poster Idea

Enlarge, decorate, and display the following poster to help students develop a sense of responsibility.

ARE YOU RESPONSIBLE?

HOMEWORK

CLEANING UP

LISTENING

CLOTHING

As children get older, we expect them to become more and more responsible. If we have high expectations for children, they learn to take responsibility and meet those expectations. Children feel empowered when expected to succeed. They take responsibility because they see new tasks as privileges. In the classroom, responsible children

- understand and accept consequences for their actions.
- complete assignments.
- clean up after themselves.
- do the "right thing."
- tell the truth.
- help others in need.
- complete a task without being asked.
- follow through without giving up.
- understand the effect they have on others.
- try to correct their mistakes.
- apologize (and mean it).

The Clean Desk Fairy

Help students become responsible for their belongings by having the "Clean Desk Fairy" visit your classroom. At the beginning of the year, explain that, from time to time, the class is visited by the Clean Desk Fairy at night. Tell students the fairy leaves treats for students who keep clean desks. Once or twice a month, check students' desks after school and leave a treat and a sprinkling of glitter on those that are in good order. (Watch out—students will check your desk too!)

MATERIALS

Strega Nona by Tomie DePaola

black construction paper

scissors

plastic spoons

permanent markers

glue

chalk

Don't Stir up Trouble

Read *Strega Nona* aloud. During discussion, ask volunteers to brainstorm how the story would have been different if Big Anthony listened to Strega Nona's directions not to touch the magic pot. Discuss the importance of following directions and taking responsibility for your actions. Give each child a piece of black construction paper, scissors, and chalk. Have each student cut a cauldron from the paper, and write one direction they always follow. Have students write their names on the spoons using permanent marker and glue them to their cauldrons. Display the cauldrons on a bulletin board entitled *Don't Stir up Trouble—Follow Directions!*

My Hands Can Make a Difference

MATERIALS

construction paper

scissors

crayons, markers

glue

bookbinding materials

Discuss the importance of caring for the earth and specific responsibilities to keep the earth clean and healthy. Distribute two contrasting colored pieces of construction paper to each student. Have students trace a hand on one piece. Ask students to cut out their tracings and draw or write one thing they can do with their hands to care for the earth. Have students glue the cutouts to the second piece of paper. Bind papers into a class book entitled *My Hands Can Make a Difference.*

I Am Responsible

MATERIALS

writing paper

Have each student fold a piece of paper lengthwise to make three columns. Have students label the first column *Responsibility*, the second *Consequence*, and the third *Privilege*. Have students list personal responsibilities in the first column. In the second, ask them to list a consequence for each responsibility if it is not met. For example, if a student writes *Set the table* in the first column, he or she might write *No T.V. for a week* in the second. In the last column, have students write privileges they sometimes receive for completing their responsibilities, such as *Allowance* or *Have a friend spend the night.* Invite volunteers to share their lists. As a class, discuss the importance of "following through" and being responsible.

Responsibility	Consequence	Privilege
1. SET THE TABLE.	1. NO T.V FOR A WEEK.	1. ALLOWANCE.
2. WALK THE DOG.	2. NO SATURDAY SWIM.	2. HAVE A FRIEND SPEND THE NIGHT.
3. DO HOMEWORK.	3. EXTRA HOMEWORK.	3. 30 MINUTES ON THE INTERNET.

Job Squads

At the beginning of the year, have students brainstorm jobs they
can do to keep the classroom safe and efficient. (Jobs could
include recycling manager, class librarian, mail deliverer, chalkboard specialist, counter cleaner, center straightener, paper collec-
tor, art supply monitor, coatrack cleaner, and floor inspector.) List
jobs on the chalkboard. As a class, narrow the list to ten job
descriptions. Have students role-play responsible completion for
each job. Display job titles and student names on a Job Squads
bulletin board (see below). Every week, assign each job to a squad
of three students. For each job squad, choose an inspector. Every
day, have each job squad complete their task while the inspector
monitors their work. Change job assignments each week, and post
changes on the bulletin board.

Save Our Planet

MATERIALS

The Big Book for Our Planet edited by
Ann Durell, Jean Craighead George, and
Katherine Patterson

butcher paper

crayons, markers

Read aloud *The Big Book for Our Planet*. Discuss each person's
responsibility to the earth and helpful actions he or she can perform. As a class, brainstorm eight or nine major environmental
problems; write each on a separate piece of butcher paper. Divide
students into groups and send each group to a different paper.
Invite groups to discuss their problems and invent a creative,
original product or service to solve them. Have each group draw
their product or service on the butcher paper. Ask each group to
share their solution. Display the papers. Have the class consider
each solution and vote for Environmental Responsibility Winners
in categories such as Most Original, Most Economical, Most
Interesting, Most Realistic, Funniest, or Best Design. (Be sure each
group receives an award.)

"Caught You" Box

MATERIALS

shoe box with a lid

paper slips

treats (stickers, candy, free time, computer time)

Discuss the definition of *responsibility*. Write a student-generated definition for the word on a shoe box. Place the box on your desk. Whenever a student displays responsibility such as remembering a whole week's homework, taking care of supplies, checking work, or completing a difficult task, place his or her name on a paper slip in the box. At the end of the week, draw five names. Invite those five students to enjoy a treat, free time, or computer time. Empty the box and begin again the next week.

Responsibility Lighthouse

MATERIALS

Keep the Lights Burning, Abbie by Peter and Connie Roop

paper towel tubes

shoe boxes

art supplies (construction and tissue paper, yarn, cellophane, aluminum foil, glue)

modeling clay

tempera paint

paintbrushes

Read *Keep the Lights Burning, Abbie* aloud. Discuss the tremendous responsibility Abbie had for her family and the sailors who depended on the small Maine lighthouse. Discuss birth order and how it can affect responsibility in a family. Ask, *What responsibilities do you have at home? at school? to friends? Are there jobs or chores you have that your older or younger brothers or sisters do not? What are they? What chores are forming you into a responsible person? How?* Distribute a paper towel tube, shoe box, art supplies, clay, paint, and a paintbrush to each student. Invite students to use the materials to create their own "responsibility lighthouse." Have students write one responsibility they have on the "lighthouse tower" (paper towel tube). Display lighthouses under the heading *We're Lighting the Way to a Responsible Future!*

WE'RE LIGHTING THE WAY TO A RESPONSIBLE FUTURE.

I SET THE TABLE

Helping At Home

Have students tell one thing their parents still do for them that they could do for themselves, such as tie their shoes, make their beds, or pick up their toys. Have each student write a parent letter asking for permission to do that thing for a week. At the end of the week, have students give oral reports detailing their experiences, successes, and obstacles. Discuss the good feelings that come from taking responsibility for new things.

Classroom Garden

Discuss the responsibility it takes to tend a flower garden. Explain that beautiful flowers are the reward for responsibility and hard work. Cover a classroom wall with a large piece of light-blue butcher paper. Label the paper *How Does Our Garden Grow? With Responsibility!* With permanent marker, write students' initials on beans. Give each student his or her bean (to represent a flower seed). When a student shows responsibility in class, invite him or her to glue the bean to the bottom of the paper. When the bean is glued, give the student three brown yarn strands to represent roots. Invite the student to glue all three strands below the bean when he or she performs another responsible act. After yarn is attached, provide the student with a green construction-paper stem. Have him or her glue the stem above the bean after a third responsible act and then receive a construction-paper flower. Have the student glue a flower to the stem when he or she performs a fourth responsible act. Soon the wall will be covered with a beautiful garden!

Compassion/ Kindness

empathizing with others and acting on those feelings with care and concern

Poster Idea

Enlarge, decorate, and display the following poster to help students show compassion and kindness.

Compassion for others, friends or strangers, is a character trait everyone needs. When children feel compassion and express it through kindness, they make themselves better people and the world a better place. Kind, compassionate children

- recognize and express appreciation for others' talents and skills.
- put others' needs before their own wants.
- help others because they *want* to, not because they *have* to.
- listen and provide a "shoulder to cry on."
- show kindness without expecting rewards.
- tell and show others they care.
- share.
- recognize and help those less fortunate than themselves.

MATERIALS

student journals

Kindness Is Catching

As a class, brainstorm things you can "catch," such as a fish, ball, train, or the chicken pox. Invite students to catch something that is not on the list—kindness. Ask students to perform an act of kindness in class each day for a week. Ask students to describe their acts in a daily journal. At the end of the week, invite volunteers to read journal entries. As a class, decide if kindness is "catching" and what can be done to continue kindness throughout the year.

MATERIALS

The Giving Tree by Shel Silverstein

tree branch

large can or bucket

plaster of paris

toothbrushes, combs, barrettes, or other toiletries

string

Classroom Giving Tree

Read *The Giving Tree* aloud. Ask students why they think the author repeated the phrase *and the tree was happy* throughout the book (to show that happiness comes from giving kindness as well as receiving it). Make a classroom "giving tree" by placing a tree branch in a large can or bucket and holding it in place with plaster of paris. Invite students to donate new toothbrushes, combs, barrettes, or other toiletries and tie them to the tree branches with string. Ask a representative from a homeless shelter to speak with the class. Afterward, have the class present the tree to the guest speaker.

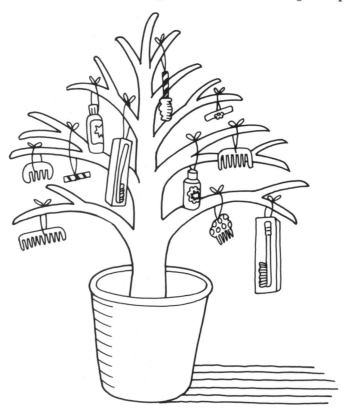

Journal Pals

MATERIALS

student journals

When introducing formal letter writing, invite students to turn their daily journals into letters to partners. Write partners' names on a posted list. Ask students to write friendly letters, discussing positive issues, offering praise, and discussing extracurricular activities. Assign new partners each week until the letter-writing unit is complete.

Sweet Seat

MATERIALS

comfortable chair

Provide a comfortable chair for the classroom and label it *Sweet Seat*. Once or twice a week, choose a person to sit in the seat. Invite volunteers to share compliments about the person in the Sweet Seat, giving examples of the person's good qualities. To develop students' listening and speaking skills, limit Sweet Seat sessions to one or two minutes. The time limit encourages students to "think on their feet" and listen carefully.

MATERIALS

red, pink, and purple construction paper

scissors

class lists

Have a Heart!

Invite students to cut out red, pink, or purple hearts during the month of February, one for each student in the class. Give a class list to each student. Each day, have students write a kind note to a different classmate and secretly put it on his or her chair. Ask students to check off names on their class lists to keep track of notes they have written.

MATERIALS

Exit with Kindness

As students leave the room at day's end, ask each to share one nice thing someone did for him or her and one nice thing he or she did for someone else. Shake each student's hand as they exit, and say, *Thanks for being kind today!*

Pass It On

MATERIALS

paper slips

basket

Write each student's name on a separate paper slip and place it in a basket. On ten other strips, write the word *me*, and place those in the basket as well. Have the class form a circle. One at a time, have each student take a slip from the basket. If a student pulls a name, ask him or her to compliment the person whose name is on the slip. If a student draws the word *me*, have him or her compliment him- or herself. Continue play until each student receives a compliment from another person.

Kindness Puzzles

MATERIALS

desktop name tags

large tagboard rectangles

writing paper

markers

scissors

manila envelopes

Provide each student with a desktop name tag and large tagboard rectangle. Assign a number to each student. Make an answer key by writing each student's name and number on a piece of paper. Have students write their numbers on the back of their rectangles and name tags. Invite students to cut the rectangles into ten puzzle pieces and place their name tags near the pieces. Have the class rotate from rectangle to rectangle ten times. During rotation, have students choose a puzzle piece and write a compliment about the person who owns the puzzle. (Students consult name tags for puzzle ownership.) Compliments should be specific, offering "clues" to the identity of the puzzle owner, such as *You are a great speller* or *I loved the story you wrote about the talking mouse.* When all ten pieces are marked, have students place their puzzles in a manila envelope numbered to match their puzzles. Place the envelopes and answer key in a learning center. Invite students to complete the puzzles and guess who owns them.

MATERIALS

books about kindness or compassion, such as *Best Friends Sleep Over* by Jacqueline Rogers

Nugget and Darling by Barbara M. Joosse

filmstrips, videos, and tape-recorded books about kindness or compassion

Let's Do Lunch!

On a designated day each week, invite several students to have lunch in your classroom. (Rotate students each week.) Ask students to bring a note from their parents giving permission to spend lunchtime in the classroom. Divide students into pairs. Provide each pair with a book about kindness or compassion. Invite students to eat, read, and enjoy each other's company. From time to time, read aloud, show a filmstrip or video, or play a tape-recorded book. To close each lunch, invite students to share what they learned from the books about kindness and compassion.

MATERIALS

A Chair for My Mother by Vera Williams

jug

label

pennies

Pennies from Heaven

Read *A Chair for My Mother* aloud. Discuss the significance of helping another person and the sense of accomplishment the giver feels when helping. As a class, choose a charity such as the Red Cross, a homeless shelter, or any other nonprofit group. Place a large jug labeled *Pennies from Heaven* in the classroom. Invite students to place pennies in the jug for three or four months. Count the pennies as a class, and invite a representative from the chosen organization to come in and receive the gift.

Who Heard a Good Idea?

MATERIALS

Anytime students complete work in small groups, have them report what they heard. Instead of asking, *Who has a good idea?*, ask, *Who* heard *a good idea?* or *Who* heard *something interesting?* By having students answer these questions, several benefits emerge. Students' listening and cooperative skills improve. They have a wonderful opportunity to model kindness. Creativity increases as outgoing students share creative ideas from the more introverted, reflective thinkers. Speaking skills improve because sharing others' ideas rather than their own tends to be less intimidating.

Compliment Can

MATERIALS

two coffee cans

self-adhesive or construction paper

craft sticks

permanent marker

Cover a coffee can with paper and label it *Compliment Can*. Write each student's name on a craft stick and place it in the can. Each day, take a stick from the can. Invite the person whose name is on the stick to stand. Ask three students to share compliments about that person. Place the person's name in a second can until all names have been drawn.

MATERIALS

Way to Go, Cocomoe!

Whenever a student gives an outstanding answer, chant, *Way to go, Cocomoe!* twice. Initiate the chant by saying the sentence once. Then invite the rest of the class to chime in for the second round.

MATERIALS

Kindness Bingo Card reproducible
(page 83)

overhead projector and transparencies

"kindness candies"
(Sweet Tarts, conversation hearts)

Kindness Bingo

Photocopy and distribute a Kindness Bingo Card to each student. As a class, brainstorm 16 synonyms for the word *kind,* such as *affectionate, good-hearted, compassionate, sweet, good, sympathetic, gentle, friendly, generous, gracious, amiable, sweet-tempered, good-natured, tender, loving,* and *neighborly.* Display the words on the overhead projector. Have students write each word in random order on their cards. Distribute Sweet Tarts, conversation hearts, or other "kindness candies" for Bingo markers. Choose a student caller, and help him or her read words aloud and mark them on a card to keep track. Have the rest of the class play Bingo. The first student to get four in a row (across, down, or diagonally) calls out, *Kindness!* Help that student read back the row of words to the caller. After three or four games, invite students to trade cards and play again.

Kindness Bingo Card

MATERIALS

tote bag

fabric paint

writing paper

Totally Terrific Me Bags

Decorate a tote bag with the words *Totally Terrific Me!* Place a letter inside asking parents to place an item in the bag that shows why their child is special. Items could include photographs, school work, at-home talent examples, or any special item. Invite parents to attach notes explaining the items and why their child is special to them. Send the bag home with each student for one night. Ask students to return the bag the next day. Invite each student to unload the bag, tell why the item was sent, and read the attached note. Ask students how they feel when someone tells them they are special.

MATERIALS

construction-paper circles

bag

tape

The Very Hungry Caterpillar by Eric Carle

construction paper

tempera paints

paintbrushes

Caterpillar of Kindness

Draw a caterpillar head on a circle and hang it on the wall. Write a kind action on separate paper circles, five for each student. Actions could include *Sharpen someone's pencil* or *Give up your place in line*. Place circles in a bag. Each day for a week, invite students to take a circle and perform the action that day. After students perform the actions, have them write their names on the circles and tape them on the wall behind the caterpillar head. At the end of the week, read *The Very Hungry Caterpillar* aloud. Invite students to paint a picture of themselves as a butterfly. Display the pictures near the caterpillar, and add the heading *Our Caterpillar of Kindness Turned into a Butterfly of Beauty!*

The Golden Rule

MATERIALS

gold construction-paper strips

Read aloud and explain the meaning of "the golden rule"—treat others the way you want to be treated. Give each student two gold construction-paper strips. Have each student write *It's cool to follow the golden rule* on the strips' fronts and his or her name on the backs. Ask students to keep the strips until they witness someone following the golden rule. Have students present the first strip to the person they witnessed performing the kind act, and then repeat the activity with the second strip. Ask students to keep the strips they receive. At the end of the week, have students count their strips. As a class, discuss how everyone can become better golden-rule followers in and out of the classroom.

The Rock

MATERIALS

large rock

acrylic paint

paintbrushes

Bring in a large rock and place it in a corner of the classroom. Discuss how a rock sometimes represents strength. Explain that it is possible to be both kind and strong, and that kindness is not a sign of weakness. Invite students to share names of people who are both kind and strong, and how they have demonstrated these qualities. Tell [students] that the rock will remain in the classroom as a reminder [of everyone's kindness.] Whenever a student perform[s a kind act, they may] paint a decoration and [write their name o]n the room until [it runs o]utside for the whole s[tudents explai]n why they paint[ed]

Handwritten note: Brainstorm about 10 caring acts / when children get to sign all ten they do butterfly / Pick Butterfly pattern w/ their face

MATERIALS

sentence strips

markers

Caring Words

As a class, brainstorm words that convey compassion, such as *love, caring, cooperation, understanding,* and *patience.* Write each word on a sentence strip. Each day, display one of the words on the chalk tray. Ask students to give examples of times when they saw a classmate exhibit this behavior. Challenge each student to put the word in action sometime during the day. At the end of the day, ask each student to report his or her actions.

MATERIALS

books

Polaroid camera and film

glue

8 ¹/₂" x 11" (21 cm x 27.5 cm) construction paper

plastic page protectors

tape

paint pens or permanent markers

Compassion Photo Frames

Discuss the need for compassion for people who are sick, such as those in nursing homes. Plan a visit to a nursing home, asking the administrator to pair each student with a resident who enjoys the company of children. During the visit, invite students to spend time reading stories and talking with their partners. Take a Polaroid photo of each pair. Back in class, have students glue their pictures in the center of a piece of construction paper. Invite students to use paint pens or permanent markers to draw photo borders around the picture. Have students cover the construction paper with plastic page protectors. Deliver the photos to the residents of the nursing home, or have students make a return trip and present the photos themselves.

Perseverance

continuing toward a goal despite obstacles

Poster Idea

Enlarge, decorate, and display
the following poster to remind
students to persevere.

Perseverance is a quality necessary for success in school, a career, and life itself. When children learn to work toward a goal no matter the "roadblocks," they become stronger, more responsible individuals. Children who demonstrate perseverance in the classroom

- complete challenging tasks.
- have a positive attitude.
- have individual opinions.
- encourage others.
- remain steadfast despite others' comments.
- lead by example.
- stand by their decisions.

MATERIALS

A Big Mistake by Lenore Rinder

Mistake Paper reproducible (page 89)

crayons, markers

A Big Mistake

Read *A Big Mistake* aloud. Discuss how the character in the story turned her "mistake paper" into a beautiful picture. Explain that everyone makes mistakes and it is what we do with mistakes that makes us successful. Distribute reproducibles and crayons or markers. Explain that the story's character made another "mistake" and needs help to fix it. Invite students to turn the "mistake papers" into beautiful pictures. Display pictures under the heading *A Mistake Can Be a Beautiful Thing!*

MATERIALS

Leo the Late Bloomer by Robert Kraus

two jump ropes

markers

index cards

Blooming Like Leo

Read *Leo the Late Bloomer* aloud. Have students share times when they desperately wanted to accomplish something and finally did. Choose one common experience, such as learning to ride a bike, and write it on an index card. Make a class Venn diagram on the floor by creating two large intersecting circles with jump ropes. Write *My Struggle* on an index card and place it in the left circle. Place the index card displaying students' common experience under *My Struggle*. Write *Leo's Struggle to Read* on a second card and place it in the right circle. Where the circles intersect, place a card that reads *Both*. As a class, compare the struggles. Write comparisons on index cards, and invite volunteers to place them in the correct place on the diagram.

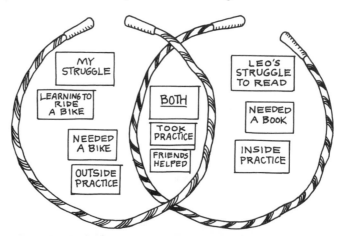

Mistake Paper

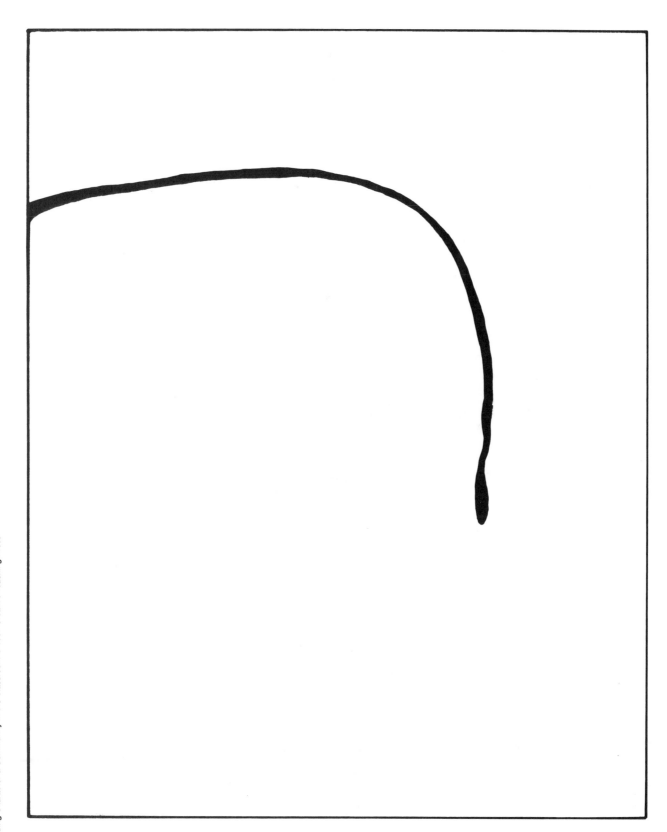

Keep on Trying!

To encourage individual students to persevere, offer *Keep on Trying!* messages and bookmarks. Photocopy and cut out several messages and bookmarks from the reproducible. Keep them in your desk. Whenever a student needs a boost, secretly place a message in his or her desk, on the chair, or in his or her coat pocket. Personalize the bookmarks and place them inside math, reading, social studies, or science books.

MATERIALS

chart paper

markers

Like Riding a Bike!

Discuss learning to ride a bike. Have students share what they need before successfully riding alone. Examples include training wheels, someone to hold the bike, practice, or a hill's incline. List responses on chart paper. Discuss how learning in school compares to learning to ride a bike. For each bike-riding example, have students think of a learning-in-school comparison. For example, training wheels could be compared to learning to count by ones before skip-counting by twos. Write the learning-in-school examples next to the bike-riding examples. Post the chart. Whenever students feel challenged and want to quit, refer to the chart and remind them that learning in school is like learning to ride a bike.

HOW IS LEARNING TO RIDE A BIKE LIKE LEARNING IN SCHOOL?	
training wheels	learning to count by ones before skip counting by twos
someone to hold the bike	teacher
practice	homework
hill	test

I know you're trying... Keep up the good work!

Working on _____ can be tough. Don't give up!

YOU CAN DO IT! DON'T THROW IN THE TOWEL!

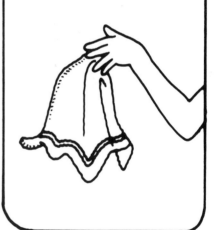

Keep this in your book as a reminder that I believe in YOU!

On the Slide

MATERIALS

gift-wrapped box

treats (candy, pencils, stickers)

Place treats in a gift-wrapped box. Take the box outside and place it on top of the slide. Tell the class there are treats for them in the box if they can get the box down. Explain rules for retrieving the box: *No one's feet may leave the ground. No person may touch the box until it reaches the ground. Any item or combination of items in the classroom may be used to retrieve the box, but they may not be thrown or broken.* Invite students to brainstorm ways to retrieve the box. Invite students to make attempts until the box comes down. Pass out the treats. Discuss how the activity relates to the concept of perseverance. Ask questions such as *Was it easier or harder to persevere when you knew there would be a reward at the end? Why? What are some other activities you participate in that require perseverance? What kinds of rewards does perseverance in those activities bring?*

MATERIALS

chart paper

markers

books and information about world-class athletes

older-student or adult volunteers (optional)

e-mail addresses

computer with e-mail capabilities

World-Class Dreams

As a class, brainstorm and list qualities of world-class athletes on chart paper. Divide the class into groups of three. Invite each group to choose a world-class athlete such as Jesse Owens, Michelle Kwan, Kerri Strug, or Oscar De La Hoya. Give each group books and information about their athlete. Ask each group to read about the athlete and find examples of his or her perseverance. (If students are very young, have an older-student or adult volunteer read to each group.) Help each group compose an e-mail letter to their athlete. Invite groups to include questions and any other personal information. Help each group send their letters. For e-mail addresses and information about Olympic athletes, use the internet address:

http://www.olympic.org/acog/newtop/dnewtop.htm

Let's Do It!

Read *Oh, The Places You'll Go* by Dr. Seuss. After story discussion, have students fold a piece of construction paper into fourths and write *I can do it!* in the center. Inside each square, ask students to draw or write one thing they want to accomplish in their lifetime and what they will do to accomplish it. Invite each student to share and explain one square. Display the papers on a bulletin board entitled *Let's Do It!*

MATERIALS

Oh, The Places You'll Go by Dr. Seuss

construction paper

crayons, markers

Three Cheers for Tacky

Read *Three Cheers for Tacky* aloud. Discuss the importance of trying no matter the situation. Invite students to close their eyes and think of a time when they felt like Tacky. Ask volunteers to share experiences. Distribute construction paper, wallpaper or fabric scraps (for Tacky's shirt), scissors, crayons or markers, and glue. Invite students to make their own Tacky (with a white breast). On Tacky's breast, have students draw a picture of a time when they had to persevere. Display the penguins on a bulletin board entitled *Three Cheers for Trying!*

MATERIALS

Three Cheers for Tacky by Helen Lester

black, white, yellow, and orange construction paper

wallpaper or fabric scraps

scissors

crayons, markers

glue

Make a Plan

Just before the end of a grading period, invite students to think about their progress both academically and socially. Distribute a Self-Assessment reproducible to each student. Invite students to complete the *How I Did* portion of the sheet. Discuss perseverance as it relates to school achievement. Invite volunteers to name one subject or work habit listed in which they want to improve most by the next grading period. Explain that the first step to improving is making a plan. Ask students to consider each subject area and work habit listed and then circle a picture to represent their plan to improve in that area. Send Self-Assessments home with report cards. Invite students to share the assessments with their parents. Remind students of their plans throughout the next grading period.

Perseverance Projects

Over two or three days, hold a personal interview with each student. Complete a Perseverance Project reproducible for each student during the interview. Ask questions one through four, and leave the Project Record blank. (Students will complete it at home.) Write a letter asking parents to help students complete their perseverance projects. In the letter, explain that the project will not only help students learn about a subject in which they are interested, it will help them gain problem-solving and perseverance skills. Send home the reproducibles and letters. Ask students to return their projects in three weeks. When projects are returned, invite students to share their projects with the class and explain what they learned about the subject and perseverance.

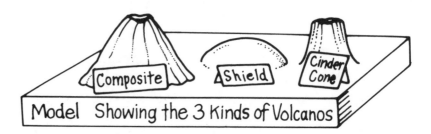

Self-Assessment

School Work

How I Did	My Plan to Improve
Reading ☺ 😐 ☹	Read at home. Read during free time.
Writing ☺ 😐 ☹	Slow down. *Aa Bb* Use neat penmanship.
Math ☺ 😐 ☹	Ask for help. − × ÷ + Study my facts.
Spelling ☺ 😐 ☹	Use a dictionary. Study at home.
Social Studies ☺ 😐 ☹	Pay attention. ? Ask questions.
Science ☺ 😐 ☹	LOG Finish projects. Work with the group.

Work Habits

How I Did	My Plan to Improve
Organization ☺ 😐 ☹	Straighten up every day. Slow down.
Working with Others ☺ 😐 ☹	Listen. 1ST 2ND Take turns.
Working Alone ☺ 😐 ☹	Stay in my seat. Work quietly.
Effort ☺ 😐 ☹	Ask for help. Finish my work.

Perseverance Project Record

Interview

1. What is one subject you would like to know more about? _____

2. What is one question you have about the subject? _____

_____

3. How can you find the answer to your question? _____

_____

4. How can you share your answer? Circle one project.

video   poster   speech   story   model   experiment   other

- -

Project Record

1. Project Name: _____

2. Date Completed: _____

3. Helpers' Names: _____

4. How I Found the Answer: _____

_____

_____

5. What Surprised Me Most about the Subject: _____

_____

6. Hardest Part of the Project: _____

7. Why I Kept Working During the Hardest Part of the Project: _____

_____

Student Signature: _____

Helper Signature: _____

Building Character & Community in the Classroom © 1997 Creative Teaching Press